Bells

poems by

Rodger LeGrand

Finishing Line Press
Georgetown, Kentucky

Bells

ACKNOWLEDGMENTS

Versions of some of the poems in this collection appeared in the following
literary journals: *The Ravens Perch, Plants and Poetry Anthology, Unlikely
Stories, The Decadent Review, Lowell Review, Evening Street Review,
Pangyrus,* and *Within and Without.*

Special thanks to Barbara Bergman, Robbin Stratton, Dimitri Kaufman,
the Ravens Perch Team, Paul Marion, Jamie Nix, Jonathan Penton, Cynthia
Bargar, Gracie DeSantis, Michael VanRooyen, Timothy Erickson, Don
Monaghan, Abby, Sophie, CC, Scott, Billy, Gracie, my parents—Charles and
Karen LeGrand, and to Ani.

Publisher: Leah Huete de Maines
Editor: Christen Kincaid
Cover Art: iStock.com/ANGHI
Author Photo: All the Kitties
Cover Design: Elizabeth Maines McCleavy

Order online: www.finishinglinepress.com
also available on amazon.com

Author inquiries and mail orders:
Finishing Line Press
PO Box 1626
Georgetown, Kentucky 40324
USA

Contents

Bells

It's cold again. The ink in my pen
has frozen. I'll need to write
the rest of this in blood.
Open my wrist with a fist
full of dead pens.
If sadness has a color
it would be the color of the universe,
which is the color of ink just as my pen
is about to run out. Faded,
meaningless words have no purpose,
and these days most words
mean anything anyone wants,
which means they mean nothing at all.
Mean is the average of things,
so maybe they mean something
half the time, except the mean words,
which always ink blot their mark.
From this corner of forever
I'm remembering Mrs. Jaroslavo
and how I didn't help her cross the street.
She was very old and told me to leave her alone.
I did. She held up traffic all on her own
and was fine doing so. If she were here now
I'd tell her that I refuse to jiggle my pen on the page
waiting for the last few words to spill out
while the traffic in my brain runs stop signs.
She wouldn't care. I'd be thankful for her indifference.
All the averages, the means and meanings,
the various ways of thinking
about the universe, are blocking
intersections and arteries and my brain cells.
Crossing points on a busy street.
Criss-cross crisis points. One strand of values slams
cold and wet into another.
The universe must have a color,
if we could step far enough away to see it.
The wind will blow through at some point
and make our bones chime like little bells.

Touch

I place my hand
on the shadow of a stranger.
I hold you like this.

They Bubble You, They Bubbled

They bubble you, they bubbled
into the bend of a neck
because love left
to empty another net
that closed around the few
silvery fish left in the bubbling seas.
They bubble you too, they bubbled back
in a wish of eyelids fluttering
like wings that will never take flight.
They fling themself
into a low tide mud bed of bubbles
with bloated wounds left
by prickly kisses
that meant nothing then,
now, or whennnnnever but
were still good to have on lonely nights.
The world is ending and they all know it.
Do you really bubble me,
they asked. Wait, but, do you really
bubble me too, they asked back.
Full throated scream as old as time,
the sound of loneliness, felt,
but too sorrowful a note for the ears to hear.
There, their, they're they say
to comfort a sea-drenched
3D-printed heart.
They is who they was
since time pressed its lazy lips
against the Sea of Tranquility
and puffed a crush of soundless waves
made tidal by the earth-moon proximity,
swished invisible foam
that folded unseen and unheard into itself
beneath the glow of celestial blue Earth,
a view from the moon, oceans
that will soon warm and swallow

continents faded from sweet grass to dirt
while they bubble, and they bubble back,
while they embrace
along the new, flooded coasts,
eyes closed, hoping for one last kiss,
hoping to love and to be loved
before it all goes under.

Zero

Nothing.
Empty sky
after the rain stops,
lungs drop, breathing
stops. There's a still moment
when zero is nothing
and everything.
Infinite nothingness.
A never-ending circle
that forever loops
itself in a loop of itself.
I'm sure I still see you
sometimes. Every silhouette
yours. Every face your face.
Infinite circles of you
repeating infinitely. Every face
loops into your face
not looking back at me,
forever faces, negative spaces,
shadow after shadow after shadow,
a never-ending circle
that laces zeros with itself within
itself within itself.
I'll look for you there
in that darkness.

Plastic

Fingerprints cloud
an hourglass.
Plastic bottle islands
drift through the Pacific.
Dried cracks in dirt where lakes
once puddled into drinkable water.
Old tires sunken into microplastic river bottoms
that get flushed into countless
private and public toilets
then flushed out to the sea.
Glowing coastal buildings,
shipping vessels docked—night
brighter than ever
in night's dark history.
Dolphins strangled by plastic netting.
Milk crates obstructing
the stomachs of walruses.
Our species is coming to its end.
Proof we were here:
Plastic fingerprints
on eternity's hourglass.

Tangerines

My ribs are the spines
of worn notebooks.
I'm wasting away to tendons
and bones scraped dry
across blue-lined pages
faded from decades of waiting
for words to fill my parchment skin.
The sound of me chewing the pages
of the notebooks that consumed me
as I now consume them, because
I am hungry and need
to find a way to survive.
And still, I choke on laughter,
at the seriousness
with which you take yourselves.
My sadness passes for tangerines
when I face you. Sunlight drapes
rectangles on the morning.
A bowl of tangerines between us. A bowl of judgement:
breath fogs a window, late
summer, just before autumn. A huff
in the search for words
that neither want to speak,
a huff of mystery that coats from the outside, a rind
to be peeled as I look out at the world
as the person I thought I was
while realizing this other thing
is the person I actually am.
Tangerines in a bowl
on the coffee table.
Sadness and judgement
in a bowl on a coffee table.
I am the tangerines.
I am the bowl holding them.
My ribs, spines of dead notebooks
being crushed by tangerines.

I'm waiting to be buried,
to bury myself in words, in ink,
starbursts of acidic citrus peels,
like a bared soul opened
with the edge of a thumb nail,
peeled away, and then emptied.

Thee People of Thee Peopling Planet

You can all fuck off, said the trees
to thee peoples. Yes,
fuck off, indeed, the coral said
before bleaching scleral white
under miles of microplastic guppies
in a microplastic sea
on a microplastic planet
that will one day soon
burn off thee
plastic people
that invented thee plastic
in thee first place.
Fuck off, from the bumble bees,
polar bears, bats. An endless
spiraling chorus of fuck off,
fuck off, fuck off
from a list of species
that have been deforested,
desalinated, destroyed.

Zombified

Waltzing through entropy.
Lost in yourself
on a peak in the Poconos.
It's been years since your neurons
started to rot like an old grape vine
wrapped around a pergola.
Swallowed up, you called it.
Unable to read or write or think or dance.
If we're not dancing, we're not mobile
and oh, immobility.... You wrote
to me one last time, knowing it was coming,
to say goodbye, that you would likely be
full-on zombified by the end of summer
and would never again writethinkbe.
I hope you're wrong
and that I'll hear from you any minute.
The old joke you told
(and wrote). In the good life
you plant seeds and get a vegetable.
In the bad life, you plant the vegetable.
I'll go out today and pull the last
of the tomatoes from the garden.
The season is coming to an end
and the last light is reddening the few leaves
that still cling to their branches. Winter's journey
will soon begin. In my mind
you're still on that mountain top
and it'll snow soon.
That's where I'll leave you.

Stone

—for Osip Mandelstam

Mortar grinding
into pestle,
the blunt edge of a memory
that awakes to itself
in the morning as it did
the previous morning
and all the others before that.
Stone-frozen chips
of frostbitten flesh skip
across the Black Sea
and sink like tossed pebbles,
lost wishes, a sea burial of history's
regard for human dignity.
War. Money. Land. Empire.
Even through the soup
of selfish prayers
drooling from blood-filled
mouths, we can still hear you
saying, "goodbye."

2023

Each syllable
a tiny noose
just large enough
to strangle an idea.

Trees

This tree, the maple, lives
only between 130 to 300 years.
That one, the Giant Sequoia,
only lives up to
3,000 years.
The Great Basin Bristlecone,
the oldest
known tree,
is thought to be over
5,000 years old.
Trees have been on the planet
about 370 million years,
humans only 3 million,
and homo Sapiens
only 300,000.
The planet isn't dying.
We are.

Sanctions

Because, sanctions
will *hit'em where'em* hurts.
Everyone this side
the Atlantic knows,
nothing matters more
than not losing money.
Human agriculture:
Lives are beans
to be counted,
then planted.

Unraveled

I thought about calling you.
Then I thought about
how the bark on the sycamore
unravels year after year
before it finally dies.
Knowing you is like
yesterday knowing
the day after tomorrow.

Throwing Dead Frogs

Imagine if Basho were born this generation
and as a kid, kept dead frogs in his pocket.
He might take one out and press
with his thumb its limp belly
to make the frog's mouth open and close.
Then, to make a splash livestreaming on TikTok,
he might speak like a ventriloquist
out the side of his mouth:
A pond, still in the morning.
Dead frog tossed in.
Sound of water.

Ongoing and Unresolved
—for Mahmoud Darwish

Over-baked media. Burned meat.
Maybe just a bite and the char
will stick to your teeth for days.
Everyone knows best. The wisdom
slithers up from behind the pale glow
of laptop light, smart phone smarties
professing the secrets of the universe
that they nor you nor I
know anything about.
And still, Shireen Abu Aqleh
shot for covering a military operation.
Crossfire sounded innocent enough
until they beat the mourners who carried her casket.
Those who pass between fleeting words
will discover more and more
with selfie stick held high to burn
like a torch of knowledge.
Blackened tongue, burned flesh
between clenched teeth.
In Mexico, Yesenia Mollinedo Falconi
and Sheila Johana García Olivera, two of many.
In 2018 in the US, Gerald Fischman, John McNamara,
Rob Hiaasen, and Wendi Winters,
all journalists at the *Capital Gazette.*
No one reads the paper anymore.
Twitter experts chirp their certainty chirps,
objectively fake baked, non-objectivity
served on a plate of 280 characters.
Shooting a journalist—almost as pointless
as shooting a poet. Yet because of their words,
they are *gone, the memories of memory.*
Take your names with you and go.

Visit: UNESCO Observatory of Killed Journalists

Worn

We break off handfuls of ocean
and peel away the plastic
with our worn fingernails.
Last spring, hotter than usual,
thousands of dead pogies
washed up on the shore,
their thin, silvery bodies
shimmering across the water's surface.
They made it to shore from the deep
without actually making it back at all.
Cradled by the tide, their bodies
rocked back and forth
the way you might put a baby to sleep.

Syracuse

Whenever I return
to the place I was born,
it rains. The stone lot
where the trailer was parked
floods. I never ratted on you,
and I never would.
No matter how hard it rains
I'll wait for you and
together we will drown.

Wheat and Sky

Fields of unmade bread
burn in Donetsk.
A man, seventies, sits in his arm chair,
wheezes through the cancer sacks
his lungs have become.
His wife, also seventies,
sits on the couch, knitting.
Their daughter, late thirties,
sits next to her mother.
She wishes she had learned
to knit, too, so she would have
something to do, to hold onto,
while waiting for the world to end.

Ritual Blessing

An invite to celebrate a life I never knew
and I was happy to join in, give thanks,
nod, and laugh at old stories of a person
who raised another person, who raised
another person I know. The line
to the casket was long. Senior family members
greeted the mourners
in a room filled with flowers.
They told stories and hugged one another.
Silent when I approached, other than a mumbled
"Thank you for coming".
When I reached the end of the line
I angled onto the kneeling bench before the casket,
made the sign of the cross,
a ritual I forgot I knew and that your family
seemed to appreciate. I found it
a comforting act, to make the cross for a purpose
and at the right time after a lifetime
of not even thinking about it.
Purposeful. In on a secret. Then I left.

Sleeping Birds

I lost you years ago, back in a time
when vines stitched across my face
to sew my lips to my eyelids.
I was younger, and it was harder
to find food, to breathe, to sleep.
We would look at each other
and imagine what a soul might feel like
if they were real or, rather,
I would look at you and you
at the shapes the stars made
along the edges of the night sky.
Your eyes bled raindrops
that smelled like left over winter
on a spring night.
I would read the patterns
in your tears the way mystics read tea leaves
to see the future and know that one day we would
crowd in on the moon before harvest,
that I might write a poem, too,
eventually, and neither of us would read it.
Without you, I use my hands as shovels,
lie down, and cover myself in earth.
There isn't anything left of you
to read, so I'll sleep until birds wake me
early in the morning
when it's my turn to leave.

Rodger LeGrand is a Pushcart nominated poet and the author of several collections of poetry, including *Studies for a Self-Portrait* (Big Table 2019) and *Two Thirds Water* (Flutter Press 2018). His first short collection of poetry, *Various Ways of Thinking About the Universe*, was published in 2005 by Finishing Line Press. His poems have appeared in many literary journals, including *Evening Street Review, Cortland Review,* and *Boston Literary Magazine.* He has taught writing at MIT and the University of Pennsylvania. Currently he designs humanitarian education courses at the Harvard Humanitarian Initiative.

www.ingramcontent.com/pod-product-compliance
Lightning Source LLC
Chambersburg PA
CBHW022104080426
42734CB00009B/1485